Only Insistence

Also by James Lindsay

Double Self-Portrait
Our Inland Sea

James Lindsay

Only Insistence

icehouse poetry
an imprint of Goose Lane Editions

Edited by Jim Johnstone.
Page design by Julie Scriver.
Cover design by Erin Russell.
Printed in Canada by Coach House Printing.
10 9 8 7 6 5 4 3 2 1

Library and Archives Canada Cataloguing in Publication

Title: Only insistence / James Lindsay.
Names: Lindsay, James, 1982- author.
Description: Poems.
Identifiers: Canadiana 20230201849 | ISBN 9781773103044 (softcover)
Classification: LCC PS8623.I524 O55 2023 | DDC C811/.6—dc23

Goose Lane Editions acknowledges the generous support of the Government of Canada, the Canada Council for the Arts, and the Government of New Brunswick.

Goose Lane Editions is located on the unceded territory of the Wəlastəkwiyik whose ancestors along with the Mi'kmaq and Peskotomuhkati Nations signed Peace and Friendship Treaties with the British Crown in the 1700s.

Goose Lane Editions
500 Beaverbrook Court, Suite 330
Fredericton, New Brunswick
CANADA E3B 5X4
gooselane.com

For Eli and Nicole

There is no such thing as repetition. Only insistence.
— Gertrude Stein

Contents

Amongst the Narcissuses

Amongst the daffodils

> I dance
> the dance
> of the involuntary
> reflection caught

> mid-glance

> apprehensive but still
> as obvious as oxygen

evading apprehension
with intimacy

> like when the clerk
> gave me my change
> and for the briefest

> of moments   held my hand
> between their opaque   latex gloves

> What a moment

to immediately move on from
> What a word

amongst

to start a poem

What a flower

daffodils

to depend upon

What a *wow*

to witness so often it begins to thin

into a gunmetal membrane

pulled over my mouth
in a depression I tolerate

yet I can't imagine privileging breath

over the tint of the spotlights'

                    dull gel

making suffocation mundane

Amongst the daffodils

                    I dance
                    the dance
                    of conceit

in an ill-lit urn of flares

                    Better it wasted away
there than thrown out on the world where

influence in this
sublimation is strutted
toward like a child

                    mountaineering
                    a rock pile pregnant
                    with snakes

Amongst the daffodils

                    I dance the dance
                    of the tallest tattletale
                    who cares not for

the life trampled
as he expresses himself

                    brutally but beautifully
                    in how honestly

he carries on

a dog on its back

snaking through grass   shamelessly
overcome

by bliss   the blast
of a homemade explosive

articulating the only way it knows   Pity the bomb

pettily ticking away
on an endless timer

Pity the sun
and its silent detonation

miming joy
afternoon after afternoon   There's a story I tell

about my mother
how she died
and another about snakes

in the rock pile
at the New Brunswick motel
by the famous giant blueberry

how the owners paid us five dollars
each to drive them out

and kill

them with sticks

Amongst the narcissuses

I sleep the sleep
of narcissists in duress

of splatters mistaken for maps   solstices mistaken

for awe

awkward awareness   obnoxious

affinity

Enough   Apologize

An apology
is only as good
as the desperation

underneath it

Imagination
like snakes   slaughtered

by the unattended

children of tourists

at a Maritime motel

Amongst rock piles
and wildflowers

children dance the dance
of serpent blood

with the manic calm
violence can educe

when life dictates life
for the first time

then ends

Amongst the forget-me-nots
the scorpion grasses   the myosotis

I dance
the dance of the projector

its spotlight

on two stories I tell:

one about my mother

and the other
about a neglected

pet rabbit

fighting through infection   pleading

for a few more moments of life

of confinement

instead of suffocating free
on a weeping
eleven-year-old's lap

And amongst the dandelions gone to seed

I dance the
dance of the eleven-
year-old entrusted

to take care of the rabbit   who forgot
to let it out

of a small cage
in a locked
mid-August room

who avoided changing

the woodchips   leading to pneumonia
and suffocating in his lap while he asked himself

if he had it in him to do it   the pillow   the pressure

and the lie

The ending
of the burden
of witness   And the shopkeeper said they knew

currency could be microscopic   And the snakes said they knew

nothing but slaughter and flight   And the rabbit could never

understand why its life was suffering   And anger became more than

fake dancing

                                        And the rabbits and
    snakes rose

to take back what should never have been given

at the hands of a child

Amongst the dandelions

                        I dance
                        the dance of a disgusted
                        mother shaking with anger
                        and stabbing eyes

To cower
in the back seat of a large car from Russia
like a cage-crazed rabbit

who hasn't had water in days   To live life in a rockpile
                                      and die by the hands of
        children

                                Hands

of the shopkeeper protected from me
and money a thing

of transit   a fair source of suspicion

        Have you seen videos
        of defensive bird maneuvers?

I'm thinking of flamingos in all their   eager-to-please splendour

a gawky   awkward
mass ascending
in a pink and black and white   splatter
                        running   taking to flight like

stitches ripping out in an immense tear

and what is a rip
but an understanding division   What is authority
                        but anxiety

        And what are stitches
        but a form of apology

Amongst the dandelion seedheads gone to puff

                        I dance the
                        dance of an oven flame

                        A performance for no one

actor as audience
a useless chorus   of echoes

repetition

                    insistence

unbridled association   We laughed

us children drunk
with dominance   It was joy
not to consider consequences

Consequences of suffering   not wearing

the glove
but also the glove   Sticks

                    It was sticks

we used to drive them out   fucking the rocks

with pine branches
older siblings took
from the barrens

Memory

Quilt construction   A playful way to consider objects

Cue azul
cue azure
cue allure
cue unconsidered
      obsession

wringing the image to solid   personal fact

Amongst the pine barrens

      I dance the dance of evasion
      circumventing the second story
      the one about how my mother died

      My mother died
      I can't speak
      as to why

Labour Day

April 22, Winnipeg

From above I saw Manitoba
Ice break apart as from above
I saw California peppered
By wildfire after a never-ending
Airport with crumpled
River lines like bunched veins
And from above cloud fields
That feel the missing more
Than your worst nights
Without the white-noise machine
And my phone breaks
You into hotel blind slats putting up
A pitiful resistance against streetlight

May 5, Demorestville

So far I've learned that this county is actually
An island that belongs to rabbits and ladybugs
And the most one could ever hope for here
Is to live each day with sleep in their eye
Sleep like a plane's shadow in retreat
From lummox clouds oafing down rainfall
Like applause for something we didn't do

May 17, Toronto

Not yet summer and cat
Burglars are active again
Inserting themselves
Into our forsaken lives
And our backyard luau plans
By not pretending they belong
To this inclination grabbing
At mid-spring manifestations
Dripping their cold ornaments
Revealing what winter did to
The infrastructure grandfathers
Claim to have had a hard time for

May 18, Vija Celmins Show at the Art Gallery of Ontario

Docents *tsk-tsk* me
As Eli yells at star-
Stabbed skies and
Chromatic splatters
Gray sandscapes
And thank you
For approaching
Photorealism
Like cloudy
Moviegoers
And thank you
For reminding me
Moving on is fear
Of where repetition
Can lead like cycles
And trance systems
Childlike schemes
Only broken
Because boredom
Was brought on
By asphyxiating
A chord of notes
Extending a lifetime
A chord of notes
Ignored because
Beauty
Friends
Is boring

May 23, New York

They've opened the retractable roof
Of the pool and from my hotel room
I watch the swimmers as I step out of
The shower in a country not of my own
In a blue cube with a button to stop
The glow and yesterday at the far end
Of the convention center
I managed moments of daylight
After an aisle seat on the way down
Landing under a storm front
And the banks of fluorescents
Clustered like cranberry bogs
Are a sorry substitute said the publicist
Your aura is yellow said the bookseller
And then for the third time that Thursday
It rained

June 8, Hamilton

In your backyard by the park
Blackberry soda from Hungary
While Eli ruined the burgundy
Hoodie you lent me because
Our star-stabbed sleeps
Are already oven guts
But thanks all the same
For making unexciting droll
And your home is beautiful
And great hosts like you better
The parts I'm uneasy sharing
And thank you for having us
Holly and Mark

June 23, Toronto

Officially summer now
And Eli you are one
And only now I see how terrible
It was before you and you
Decided to smile at me then for me
And now I am honoured to hold you
For as long as you'll let me
Before you will do what you have to
Do to become the rest of yourself

July 12, Bluewater

The rabbits have followed
Us here and with them cold
Clouds that hog the sun
And piss on Lake Huron
Thumping holes in shore
And hatching murmur circuits
Concerning an elderly couple
We passively evicted
Who hold the belief this land
Is an extension of themselves
This cottage composed of Latvian
Tchotchke handcrafts constructed
By hands that populated it
With pool noodles and water shoes
And sun hats and German-style
Board games and yellowing
Paperbacks' Bible-thin pages
Used to start cheerless cooking
Fires whose smoke weaves
Into threadbare outerwear
The cells of our hair and skin
The specs that make us up
Until we accept this new life
Until one day all of it is over
And we finally notice
The hidden room's jib door
Where we're expected to abandon
Everything without hesitation

July 14, Bluewater

It's a heinous wrong to watch wildflowers
And the surf dozing what's left of the beach
In the yard of a cottage I did not build
By hand with sons I had to fight to have
A relationship with on taken land
I say nothing on while complaining
About overkill and depleted beach
Emptied of sand and occupied by rocks
And each rock is an unimaginable failure
I don't want to say like ghosts but sure
Like ghosts the kind wished back to life
Then disappointedly wished back dead
Because the beach is easier to occupy
When we believe rocks cannot claim
And the wildflowers are canary yellow
Turnip violet and bone-china white
Because they hate us that much

July 31, Toronto

Nicole I know I apologize
Too much too often but I love you
In an intensity that scares me
In an intensity that is everyday
Exhaustingly beautiful I'm amazed
By the person you are always
Becoming and flattered to be bound
To you by life you carried and carry
In water so cold it hurts my cityboy
Skin as we cling to each other not
Only for support but because we can
And want to and Happy Birthday
To a person I am proud to have
As a permanent part of my life

August 7, Toronto

Midsummer tree sex
Lummox-soft ejaculate
Outnumbering oxygen
Coquettish and encased in
Amber but is summer still
Mid if light is in decline
And the shoe museum
Is off holiday hours
And my neighbour sells
Black market fireworks
Out of his storage unit
Prolonging his quarrel
With night-sky dullness
Poxed by ominous blips
He swears are in pursuit
Like rabbits on the rail path
The ones I saw yesterday
And the day before and the day
Before the air turned moribund
And myopic in these midday
Mornings diffusing August
Wreckage gently encasing us
In a deadening flaxen haze

August 18, Toronto

I talked to him again today
The neighbour whose name
I cannot recall whose face
I can only vaguely recollect
Whose relation has grown
Beyond nods to full-blown
Banter and last night he saw
Me putting tiny red rubber
Boots on my dog like one might
Apply a condom by candlelight
And I could tell he didn't know
What it's like to nurse a paw
Slashed by smashed glass
How the vet said to fasten
Bandages and keep Quinn
Away from the rabbits
White flowers and water
Vapour everyone's begun
To suspect at this point
And dates are a funny thing
At least when someone tells
You them because faith
Is involved and I don't
Think that you and I
Reader and writer
Have that kind of relationship
At least not when the neighbour
Aims lasers at night Boeings
Drifting above as we feign sleep
Under blips we assume won't fall

August 30, Guelph

The rabbits' eyes are red
Because they hate us
And the goose you thought
Was dead was only dying
And when the sixth-floor
Balcony door poltergeisted
Everyone blamed the wind
But later in the river park
It yoinked a bag of chips
And blew them to the goose
Wounded and dying by itself
So if I have to choose a side
I'm choosing the wind
And can't wait to know
The flurries it promises

Labour Day, Toronto

Let's be clear regarding the rabbits
And flowers I insist hate us
What I'm trying to say is that they
Are actually water vapour claiming
Not to hate the air show as much
As you but still not above sharing
In the schadenfreude but I will still miss
The red puffs snuffing out summer
With fuck-off booms rattling
Our sunburnt nerves tsk-tsking
Exhibition tchotchkes we won
Only because the carnies pitied
Our poor throws and sunburns
Witnessed by children with names
We've already forgotten and no
I don't hate the air show as much
As you but I'm still glad autumn
Has come to put down summer
Like a tender veterinarian
Who is afraid of animals
Obliviously subsisting on
Recognizing the parts of us that
Disappear when they evaporate
And some people are so exhausted
They have to live by
Dreaming terrifying clarity
Terrifying clarity as a view
Born under storm clouds
Waiting to break apart
Ice fields from above
Creeping planes and geese
Crossing plains of grease
Troughs of boiling oil
Rivers floating doughnuts
Like collapsed chemtrails

Ellipsis stuntmen dot across
A dying season's busy skies
Trying to warn us about things
That have always hated us no
They have just noticed us
And are only beginning
To discover their displeasure
Spending summer with strangers
It is impossible to learn to love

The Lake

I don't know how to talk about my biological father, so instead
I'm going to describe the lake: it's blue, with swans.
    — Tony Tost, "Swans of Local Waters"

I've never seen the other side,
but even from here, now, it's obvious
that something has caught fire, smoke
so bold it appears as sky accusing
gravity of lying, as being pointed
at by a body larger than yourself
but still familiar, the way it made
the swans deny the unimaginable
whim, fleeing from fire, refusing
to know the way life is personal,
touching one another like trees,
the trees in the forest that enfolds
the lake, the swans, where smoke
laid blame, and I don't know how
to talk about my biological father,
so instead I'm going to describe
how eventually the smoke met
precipitation, atmosphere so
severe, rain fled flight from clap
bracketing clap, spark dividing
spark, making paranoid secret
language fantasies from the far
side, where sons are born firstly,
stunted by trying to be by water.

I don't know how to talk about
my biological father, so instead
I'm going to describe the lake:
like any ancient and enigmatic
body of water, it is full of things:
collapsed algae-caked vehicles,
whose presence I can't speak to,
who've never known ownership,
like lucky dogs, living to implement
themselves upon people pretending
to remember being born, and fish,
of course, and because the lake
is acidic, it's a glass-bottom boat,
forgetting the physics of floating,
a sense of self making a window
out of roiling, churned-up water
shenanigans whipping foam into
a swan bevy, becoming cannibal
in smashed lace harassments
homesteading what, from a great
height, appears blue, but up close
is a terrifying non-colour, no, not
white, hives of migraine meadows
held in the shape the shattered
urn took on after I failed to fix it.

I don't know how to talk
about my biological father,
so instead I'm going
to describe the lake:
it's blue, with swans
fortifying their shores
by hissing at forest
embracing the waves
and sons escaping
out of fear born out
of anger or anger
born out of fear,
pulled waterside by fires
lifeguards lit to ward off
unwanted swimmers,
asking what is a fist
if not a ball of knuckles,
a den of joints,
gripping, anticipating,
curled and waiting.

I don't know how to talk about my biological father,
so instead I'm going to describe the lake by way of
describing the trees that are part of the lake in that
they are not the lake: they are green and made up
of a terrifying sharpness murmuring when I walk
through a bevy of their kind clustered like strangers
forced to stand together and practice the patience
of being thrust about while protecting themselves
with flattened palms, hissing: *sorry, sorry, sorry.*

I don't know how to talk
about my biological father,
so instead I'm going to talk
about the lake, how sky fed
aquifers before subterranean
catheters coned swan water
from a socket of shield ogling
stars frantically attempting to
communicate by constellation,
trying to ask for something
that can never be provided
and all I can say is, *Oh, look
a pattern, what does it mean
to me, and can it make money?*

I don't know how to address this talk
about my biological father or the lake,
so instead I am going describe its blue
with swans: sky masquerading as hills,
hills I've lost something in, something
on purpose forgot, threadbare, sparse
flu-like symptoms thinning out water
that at the height of its heyday wafted
parades of seafoam all cockily goose-
stepping down esplanades paved over
an old place, at least it feels old, not new
and familiar and chronic and playfully
hidden under collapses on the bottom
of what I fail, am unable to talk about.

I don't know how to address this talk
about my biological father or the lake,
so instead I am going use a placeholder
title: "The Blue Is Cold and the Swans
Are Vicious," though it irritates me
and lacks pizzazz snazzy birds hiss
at with their toothy tongues I'd rather
not think about, so instead I turn in
disgust to describe the distance
between the shores, which feels
significant and difficult to articulate;
I suppose that's why no one has ever
spoken to me about the weird way
piercing light prods the blue
temperature I've never set foot in,
but I can tell, even standing back
here, that it's low and whispered.

I don't know how to keep pretending
I know how to talk about the lake or
its swans on the blue signifying what…
the noble viciousness of fatherhood
or something like that, so instead
I want to talk about how unhurried
it softens sharp metal edges and
broken glass abandoned by design,
to be estranged from remembrance
like the lake appearing as solid ice,
like predators knowing to give off
the illusion of something dependable
while waiting to deliberately collapse.

But I know what caught fire,
the burning I've been ignoring
for several pages now, and I don't
know how to talk about my biological
father, so instead I'm going to describe
the structure: even before being a blaze,
it was never made to be lived in,
with its open air and artificial walls,
an atrium cut out of the woods
around the lake, it served as a blind
for the lifeguards to see how swimmers
swam unseen, observing their merging
wakes born confident then drifting
into timid nods, reluctantly participating
in violence that birthed them,
the vicious thrashing of water
slowly scatters bodies, floating
smoke escaping prudish gravity,
its frantic signals called quaint
by those away enough not to be
threatened yet by flame spread.

I don't know how to talk about my biological father,
so instead I'm going to describe the others: the ones
who I grew to know as owls: placeholders perching
and screeching a not-forgotten flight path running
from forest to lake, worn down by decades of steps,
but look how grass has pluckily started to return, look,
the smoke is still visible, and that is why this pathway
was stressed here: the endless running of survivors
from the burning they began to flee as children, but
by the time they reached the far shore their accounts
failed to line up the way we wanted them to: aisles
of dried pine needles between ceaseless military
parades of pine trees, and because they swam,
they're naked in a caressing world of small claws
that will always be better than where they began.

I still don't know how to talk about the biology
between my father and me, so instead I'm going
to describe the lake: sometimes the lake is the lake,
and sometimes the lake is the things that float on it
and the things that drown in it that make it what it
is: a rage of waves eroding rocks to a pebble beach,
each small stone confident in immanent restoration
that only serves to accentuate the soft gnawing away,
a way station, a well, and away from the smouldering
that both does and does not want to be extinguished.

I don't know how to talk about my father,
so instead I'm going to describe the lake
like bruised pewter with its humouring
of swans who wait to hear the yarn
again, this time absent of agreement,
the tiny histories that seed memory,
the path consuming itself, cannibal
meanderer, looping from water to water
without chance to touch green: awkward
ownership over land lending to awkward
recall: absentminded myopia and Stein
says, *There is no such thing as repetition.*
Only insistence. And insistence is missing
beneath the meniscus, the false curve
of water feigning physique it lacks as
it cries, *Why why why why*
do patterns assert in me like air
abandons the lungs of the drowning?

Only Insistence

The light stays but we can't grasp it.
We leave the tree rocking its
Head in its hands and we
Go indoors.
        — W.S. Merwin, "Vocations"

With piercing March light raking

Through clutching leafless limbs

Of the trees that were just beginning

To receive the attention they didn't

Know how to ask for before blockades

That some insisted would end everything

Didn't end anything that couldn't be

Forgotten and those who could turned

To retreat indoors to do what they do

What they thought they wanted to do

Living with so many walls and outlets

For unaccommodating imagination

To accumulate in the style of carbon

Monoxide or the virus and its way

Of wraithing from place to place

Person to person ignored at first

Then properly invisible and silent

Like anything that is learning

What it doesn't need to exist

Streets were beaches in early April

Bright and bleached and barren

Wind-whipped and not at all empty

Where some chose to linger

And some insisted because they had to

And some maintained as defensiveness

And overthought intimate gestures

Until they became meaningless shapes

Some claimed to find deep meaning in

Because for some soothing themselves

Was complicated and for some denying

Satisfaction gave them something to do

And eye contact was flocks of birds

And the way they distance themselves

From one another when two groups

Collide without contact

Like flowers in a field

Refusing to acknowledge each other

Temperate antagonism encircling

Some like gratuitous ooze

Some shunned by going into torpor

By apprehensive daydreaming

In sunlight that survived the filter

Of window glass some dared not

Lift at first but felt compelled to

Though once they did they saw

One another and were confused

About what to say and what

The consequences might be

And some were always hungry

But everything was confined

And all some did was sleep

In fretful bursts their lungs

Allowed them and were grateful

To wake to their children crying

At night and grateful

To sing them back to sleep

And then watch them breathe

As their small bodies readied

For what no one could say

Someone's grandmother died

Though she was already dead

Someone's grandfather died

Though they'd never met him

And someone's parents died

Alone and they avoided this

And some lay awake imagining

Others slowly dying until

It went quiet like wind

Reminding them to move

To keep moving and go out

Early in the morning and late

At night to take advantage

Of the solitude in the now

Perpetual dull with

Day lilies and dandelions

Demanding their way through

Asphalt and the hard cold

Ground unwilling to thaw

For the forecasted burials

So when someone said fire

We all nodded in unison

Yes fire was the way to go

Insist by fire

Distance by blank space

Prospect by cancellation

Apologize by layoff

Conserve by eviction

Defend by accruing

And making customer

Service cry on the phone

Exit by basement

Apartment light

Faith by mistrust

Perform by elaborate

Recitals of compassion

That were so common

An entire generation

Insisted novels about

Stability and legacy

And another generation

Writing about wanting

To continue to live

In the afterworld

Some couldn't unsee

What had been seen

Mistook sequences

That were once so sure

In shape and structure

In routine and meaning

Until a slow imbalance

Detached everyday

From itself mooring

Afternoon after afternoon

Folding itself in and in and

In until unrecognizable

And then for a week it rained

A low whisper and some struggled

To understand what was said

There was a general understanding

What we were hearing was manic

Morse dotted and dashed so fast

Something in the music was lost

Something that required a voice

Few got close enough

To comprehend the vocalizations

And those who did were shunned

With a gaze or a pitiful smile

That was in fact brave fear failing

To convince anyone of anything

They didn't already know so when

Voices were heard behind the fence

So many and causally close together

Some insisted they were waking up

In a movie someone told them about

It was a slatted fence allowing

Slits of vision where some saw

Dashes of colour clustering like

Flocks of birds before exploding

When an unfamiliar thing

Came close enough to be read

As a threat causing calm scatter

And infuriating passive parting

Before some could write notes

To pass through the notches

Containing details and guesses

As to what was being planned

The numbers no one wanted

To see but had to acknowledge

Some were able to watch themselves

Embracing half-remembered partners

For the first time in unfamiliar spaces

And that was so unreal

Dreaming failed

And then the wind came to touch

Everything we were told not to

Touch with its betrayal of spring

Air and an insensible summer

Touch of knowing it was watched

Touch like a whispered report heard

With bent head and hand over phone

So some couldn't read lips

So some could demonstrate knowing

The law while others freed bodies

Theirs and their form of true ghost

Dandelion pollen blown adrift

Pilfered by a loitering winter

An open window maddened

Breathing selfish exhalations

Shamelessly in front of those who

Had no choice but to be covered

Some spoke of this time

As an age of aloof children

Suspicious of others' air

Of casual contact

And close passage

Stripping cities of intimacy

Bleaching streets

Emboldening and blistering

Pedestrians and the excuses

Now required for mapping

Canyons carved by the joyful

Floods of lives that fed them

Some saw themselves as citizens

When they were really a readership

And once everything evaporated

All some had was empty and empty

Was accompanied by a spectrum

Of filters separating uninvited

Negative ellipse pitter-patter

Of a thousand footfalls fleeing

The sound of rubber bullets

Ricocheting when not impacting

Bodies that weighed danger

The normalized air pressure

Enough to crush an iron insistence

Mirror-like windows of dark cars

Some paused to affix looks in

Never knowing what mask is on

How its addition alters facial

Features some depended upon

To read if the beating was close

This is where history began again

Where some were told it insisted

Itself into a lifelike violence

Because abrasion because some

Died but there was disagreement

On how one becomes suddenly aware

That an animal is watching

Without making eye contact

Psychobabble masking misanthropy

Paranoia as misfired instinct paid

To do what it did without gusto

In the third false spring of the season

Cascading rumours murmured

About why new labour was so great

Without the outings made by design

To encourage closeness that seems

Reckless now to even imagine touch

So casual it only had to stop talking

To get lost along with the rest of it

Days insisted themselves as labour

Time insisted itself as vague

Contact insisted itself as complex

At splash pads toddlers insisted

As carnivores in an uneasy peace

And in the lot where the developer

Failed to erect rows of townhouses

Filled with unnamed constellations

Of glass and juvenile forests

Of scheming day lilies and dandelions

Teenagers insisted they were steam

Though some reported hearing night

Cries at the centre of a Venn diagram

Between fear and anger and ecstasy

Chaotic laughter accompanying shock

An epiphany of horrific knowledge so no

Not a diagram as much as a froth or foam

That insists itself upon the hands of some

Like the dollops the sensor dispenses

At elevators and entrances insisting

They weren't made to shape air as a trick

Entrepreneurship said up up

Up with you all there are some

Things worse than dying worth

Dying for and I am woven of them

See how easy the inward became it

Then some saw Utopia arriving

In the form of details obstructing

The year of slow reading

And frequent betrayals

While children hibernated

Hopscotch paths collapsed

And war began in earnest

The rain began to rain

As if acquiescing to the sky

Spilling what it was told to hold

Performing a soliloquy of empathy

The moon detesting public crying

The night air being a private thing

Refusing to discuss choreography

What the stars are up to

How they explode and reform

Explode and reform in rapid

Vibrating insistences

So suspiciously intimate

Conspiracies got lost

But the consensus was

We were coercing them to dance

As if incineration was immediate

Or what we believed to be dance

From this privileged distance

Insistence

New litter

New flock

New pattern

New insistence

New choreography

New acrid grammar

New words overturning

New horrible overtures

Initiating by fragment

Flocks in new blue

Screen's shivering static

Velcroing horizons apart

New fascist affection

In estranged absentia

So new ways to name

New dreams with teeth

Escaping gasped maws

In brimful salvos

New forms of deadfall

Wild xylophones keys

Chiming groundward

Restrained by joints

And illegal chokes

Cultural autumnal

Rhythm exposed bones

Some came to associate

With barren interiors

Barefaced skeletons

Clawing their way back

From desire in disarray

Because accountability

Because it was obvious

What made rain rain

Each droplet individual

And momentarily visible

Because collective shame

Knew this had been willed

Because acknowledged

Protection was privilege

Because the slatted fence

Became a web of nets

Because the new litter

Caught became negative

Because the negative

Was made of what

Could not be unseen

Because it obscured view

Communication ceased

Because contrails

Were intended to baffle

Because this was defensive

Manoeuvres of who could

Not request affection

Who could not be touched

Any more who could not

Be touched anymore

Who could not be touched

Anymore but who would

Have previously invited it

Who would have before

Expressed physically

Their desire in disarray

When language worked

Because it was promised

That it would work

The way it worked

When expressions

Were defenseless

Because when it came

Time to name it some

Insisted pewter

Was an agreeable

Colour to signify

Leisurely collapse

And how it feels

To learn to stand

Again and again

Insistence: Appendix

Amongst the flowers   the

daffodils   the

forget-me-nots   the wild

flowers   dandelions

gone to seed   biological

fathers   burning

smoke   water   with swimmers

Lifeguards

Sarcastic yellow   Shamefaced violet

Entitled blue   Rockpile motel   famous blueberry

all vapour   escaping

Some left

some stayed

and let it be known

Rabbits and flowers   hating us

The beaches   painfully bright

and made of rocks

and children

of rocks: sand

its unimaginable   failures   The night sky

is for fireworks   and ghosts   and air shows

                                                are warmongers

                As a child

                                        I passively tortured

a rabbit to death   and now they hate us   As a child

                        I didn't know how to talk

                        about my biological father

so instead I talked   and talked   until I thought

        I was understood

And I talked

over   and over

        and over   afternoon

                after afternoon   after afternoon

                After noon

Until Eli   and Nicole

                and Quinn
                and Holly
                and Mark   were there

though

on our own now

Then talking

didn't describe   what the trees were doing

underground   where warrens

of rabbits   safely conspired   sifting

instinct

from anxiety

blinking

out a Morse

failing to describe   what the night sky is up to   silently

as the material

world turns   against us   the hateful rabbits

the fireworks full of promises

the dancing declawed warships

the tsk-tsk tchotchkes   accruing like deadfall

how bare branches   are holding bone arms

wrapped around   us as if unsure

                            of our worth

but not wanting to lose

something it could use

Acknowledgements

"Labour Day" was originally published as a chapbook by above/ground press and an excerpt also appeared in *Dusie*. Thank you to rob mclennan for publishing it and for all your enthusiasm and commitment to writing.

"The Lake" was originally published as a chapbook by knife | fork | book. Thank you to Kirby for publishing it and for your friendship and tireless support of poetry and poets. And thank you to the editors of *CV2*, who included an excerpt in "The Daddy Issue." Thank you to Tony Tost, for writing "Swans of Local Waters," and to Heather Christle, for writing *The Crying Book*, where I found the quote. This poem would not exist without your writing.

"Only Insistence" was written in the opening months of the COVID-19 pandemic and owes a debt to the song "A dream of water," performed by Colin Stetson and Laurie Anderson, from Stetson's album *New History Warfare Vol. 2: Judges*. Thank you, Ben Ladouceur, for all your kind words and early encouragement on this one.

Thank you to Fred Wah, Susan Holbrook, and Tyler Pennock for your beautiful, generous endorsements.

Thank you to Alana Wilcox and everyone at Coach House Books for giving me a chance to work alongside great books and amazing people.

Thank you to Alan Sheppard, Martin James Ainsley, Ross Leckie, and the icehouse poetry board, and everyone at Goose Lane Editions.

Thank you to my editor, Jim Johnstone, who was instrumental in helping to shape these poems and bring them to light.

And thank you to Eli, Nicole, and Quinn, for being my everything.